Me and My Shadows

Shadow Puppet Fun
for
Kids of All Ages

Puppets by Elizabeth Adams
Revised by Bud Banis, Ph.D.

BeachHouse
Books

Copyright

Original version published as *Shadow Pictures My Children Love to Make* by Elizabeth Adams, published in 1910 by Lloyd Adams Noble.

Graphics were refurbished and text was updated by Bud Banis, Ph.D.. The updated aspects are copyright 2000 by Bud Banis, Ph.D.

Cover graphic—is an original construction by Bud Banis, Ph.D. using the concept from the original book by Elizabeth Adams.

First Printing, November, 2000

ISBN 1-888725-44-3 Regular Print BeachHouse Books Edition

Library of Congress Cataloging-in-Publication Data for regular print edition

Adams, Elizabeth.

Me and my shadows : shadow puppet fun for kids of all ages / puppets by Elizabeth Adams ; revised by Bud Banis,Ph.D..

p. cm.

Rev. ed. of: Shadow pictures my children love to make, 1910.

ISBN 1-888725-44-3

1. Shadow-pictures -- Juvenile literature. [1. Shadow pictures.] I. Banis, Bud. II. Adams, Elizabeth. Shadow pictures my children love to make. III. Title.

GV1218.S5A33 2000

BeachHouse Books   PO Box 7151   Chesterfield, MO 63006-7151
636-394-4950   beachhousebooks.com

Table of Contents

Introduction

Shadow Puppets and How to Make Them

Me and My Shadows

A Book Planned to Entertain Children of All Ages

Entertainment doesn't always have to be expensive or require elaborate equipment, When this book was first published, many thought shadow-pictures were possible only on stages where accommodations could be made for special lighting systems. This may be true for large audiences and startling effects, but shadow puppets are now among the simplest toys and tools for amusement. Lights strong enough are to be found everywhere, and the basic equipment is always at your fingertips, so to speak, or "right at hand."

Each night when you turn on your lights, you must realize that your shadow is cast behind you on the wall. Now if, instead of standing your whole body before the light, you merely hold your hand there, you will find that you have formed a shadow-picture of your hand. And if your wall paper is not a dark shade you will discover that this shadow-picture, which you make of your hand by the aid of your home light, is equally as pleasing as the shadows made by a more intense light—though, perhaps, it may not be as clearly defined. If you want to increase the "sharpness" of this shadow, you can simply stretch an ordinary sheet across the wall so that there is a marked contrast between the black shadow and the white background. An easy way is to throw a sheet over the top of the door and make your pictures on that. Any flat surface will prove satisfactory, providing, of course, your light is shining directly upon it. Generally speaking, the stronger the light and the whiter the "screen," the better the shadow picture will be!

 It doesn't matter what kind of light you use, as long as you can focus it on just one part of the wall. The rest of the room should then be darkened as much as possible. Never use two lights side by side, for then each would cast a shadow and give you a doubled picture. Always have your light strong enough to cast a sharp shadow of

1

your hands; or, if your light is weak, bring the light close enough to your hands so that the shadow is distinct.

The exact distance to hold your hands from the light in order to cast a sharp shadow can only be determined by experiment. The nearer the light you place your hand the larger will be the shadow; but the nearer the hand is held to the wall, the more distinct the shadow will be.

Forming these pictures is relatively simple. The illustrations in this book have all been specially drawn from the particular poses of children's hands. It might be difficult at first to hold your fingers in all the positions. These are probably good exercises for improving dexterity and finger control! I hope you will find each illustration self-explanatory. The poses shown here are all pretty easy, and with a little practice, can be mastered by anyone.

Shadow pictures are always available, don't cost anything, and will provide endless rainy afternoon or after dinner delight.

The Puppets

Suggestions:

 Don't forget that the sleeve must be folded back so that the bare arm casts a gracefully bending shadow which will form the swan's neck By lowering and raising the little finger of the right hand and at the same time straightening the wrist a little, it will seem as if the bird is eating. If the left hand is moved backward and forward the swan will appear to flap her wings. By moving both arms forward, the shadow will seem to "swim" away, fading from sight as the arms pass from their position before the light.

The Swan

Suggestions:

By lowering and raising your little fingers you can make the birds open and close their bills. If you tightly hold the first and second fingers of each hand with the thumb, thenraise them just enough to let the light pass through, each of the swans will then have an eye. You must be careful to keep the back of your right hand well away from the light, or the bird's head will be too fat.

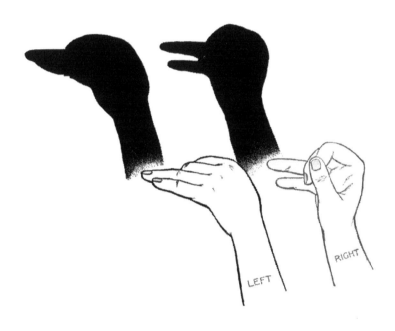

Two Ducks in line

Suggestions:

Moving your fingers in this pattern may take some practice. If it is too difficult for the fingers to hold their positions, let your little finger make the lower part of the bird's bill, and then bend your ring finger behind the second finger. To make the birds open and close their eyes, do not lower your first finger which is bent, but move your thumb back and forth to cover the opening between the first and second finger. If you let the swans peck at each other, keep your wrists stiff so that your hands will not turn and change the whole shadow-picture.

Two Ducks Talking

LEFT   RIGHT

Suggestions:

When you cross your thumbs in making the bird's head, be sure to keep the left directly above the right, For if the thumbs press straight against each other the light will then strike them both; and they will cast a shadow which will make it appear as if the bird has two heads. Keep the palms of your hands always opened towards the light. If you wave your hands, it will seem as if the bird is flying. Do not let your fingers bend so that the light can pass between them or the bird will look split down the middle.

Flying Bird

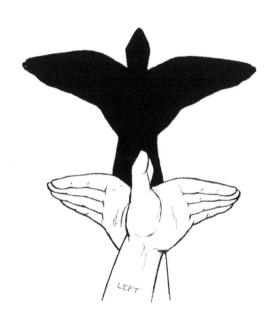

Suggestions:

In fixing your hands to make the shadow-picture of an eagle's head, bend the little finger of your left hand far enough down so that it will not cover the opening formed by the other fingers and spoil the bird's eye. Keep the fingers of your right hand together so that the light can strike only the index finger, and the line which shapes the upper part of the eagle's beak will not be wider than the lower. The left arm should always be held so close to the right that the light cannot shine between them.

Eagle Head

Suggestions:

Keep your back to the light and raise your right arm until it is level with your shoulder. The outline of the cat's body is best made by wrapping a shawl—or even a napkin—around the right arm. The ends of this shawl can then be held in place by the left hand which should grip the elbow of the right arm. Do not let the left hand come below the right elbow, or it will cast a shadow. Extend the index finger of the left band just enough so that it will form the cat's tail.

Cat with Tail

Suggestions:

Keep the little finger of your right hand bent tightly against your palm, but hold the other fingers loose—just as they are drawn. It will then be easy to make the mouth of the shadow-picture dog. Now, if you should want to force your dog to "howl," move your right hand by bending it upward from the wrist with a jerk, and at the same time lower your thumb. When you finally fix your left hand in the proper position for the picture, do not move it to make the dog close his eye — simply lower your little finger.

Puppy Head

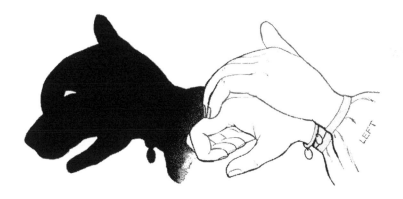

Suggestions:

If you can't hold your fingers in the way that they are drawn, change the position of your right hand. Bend all the fingers, except the thumb and little finger, against the palm. Turn your right hand over and, bending the left thumb to the palm, place your right thumb in the position which the left formerly held. The bull's horns will then be made by the shadow of the thumb and little finger of the right hand. This picture can be made only when the light shines from the left, striking your hands from the side.

Bull Head

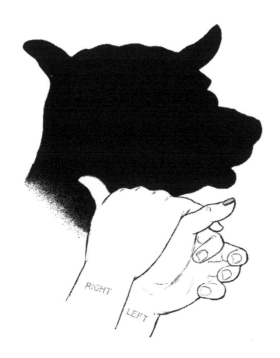

Suggestions:

The deer's nose is formed, as you see, by the first three fingers of the right hand. The best effect will be produced if these fingers are kept close together so that the light cannot strike each one and cast a shadow of three fingers. Touch the tip of the index finger to the tip of the ring finger, and then let the long second finger rest on the top of those two. Try to hold them all tight so that they will look like one big finger. You can do it. Keep the fingers that make the deer's horns straight!

Deer Head

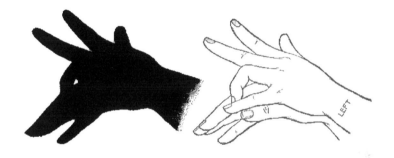

Suggestions:

Bend and straighten the fingers of the left hand, moving them in a lazy fashion to imitate the swinging of an elephant's trunk. Be sure to keep the fingers in a line behind the index finger so that the light will not strike them all and cast a broad shadow. Bending the fingers up until the tips touch the palm will make it seem as if the elephant is eating. If the thumb of the left hand does not reach out far enough, project your little finger. The elephant will then have longer tusks. Don't let the light shine between your wrists or the elephant will have a hole in his head!

Elephant

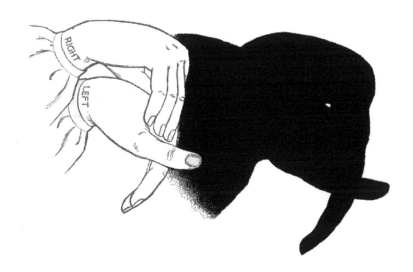

Suggestions:

The lower jaw of the horse is made by the shadow of the ring finger and the little finger of the right hand. These fingers should be held one behind the other. A handkerchief rolled up and tied around the wrists will cast the shadow of the horse's collar. To imitate the actions of a horse chewing his oats, move the fingers of the left hand slowly to make the "mouth" move. Bend your arms up and down at the elbow. This will cause the horse's head to sway in a life-like manner while he is "eating."

Horse with Collar

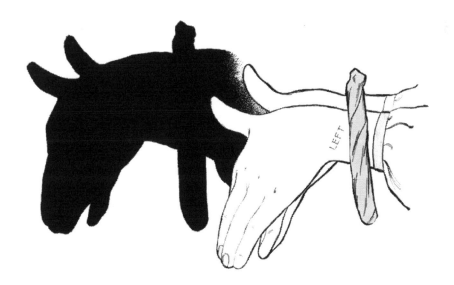

Suggestions:

The position of your head is important in this one, as the shadow of the top of your head makes the body of the duck. If you don't hold your left hand level with your shoulder, your head will cast a shadow in the wrong place. Hold the wrist of your right hand tightly against your forehead and don't use the left hand at all. The ring finger of the right hand should be held closely behind the long second finger or the light will strike them both and then the upper part of the bird's bill will be wider than the lower.

Duck Swimming

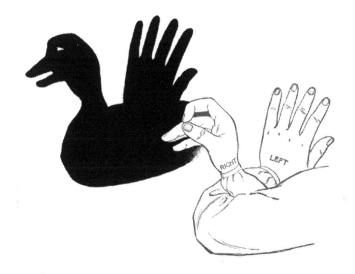

Suggestions:

An ordinary china plate should be held in the left hand to cast a shadow which will represent the shell of the snail. Keep your left hand in its fixed position and move your right arm so that the snail seems to draw back into his shell. Grip your right elbow with your left hand, then hold the plate between your thumb and elbow. The general effect is better when the shadow is made in this way. As you make the snail crawl forward, let him slowly move his horns back and forth. Do not bend your fingers!

Snail

Suggestions:

If you ever want to make a shadow-picture in the opposite direction from the drawings, just use your right hand where the left is marked, and the left where the right is marked. Compare the rabbit on the cover with the rabbit on this page! See how easy it is! By changing the positions of the shadow-pictures so that they face one another, you can have two or three little children all making pictures together with you. Let your rabbit shut his eye, move his front paws, and wave his ears.

Rabbit Body

Suggestions:

To make the picture of a wolf, the three fingers of the left hand which cast the shadow representing the nose must be held almost one behind the other—not one above the other. In this way the palm of the hand is held practically parallel with the floor. If you then just touch the tip of the index finger of your right hand to the middle joint of the long second finger of your left hand, the wolf's eye can easily be made. Stretch the thumb of the right hand forward and bend the index finger of the left hand backward.

Long-nosed Wolf

Suggestions:

If you have difficulty making the mouth of the shadow-picture goat, take away his beard. Let the little finger of the left hand form the goat's lower jaw. Hold the other three fingers close together to cast the shadow of his nose. In this way you can make an excellent shadow-picture without cramping your little finger. The first two fingers of the right hand should be stretched out very straight for they make the goat's horns—and remember not to bend them when you move your thumb to imitate the twitching of the goat's ear

Goat

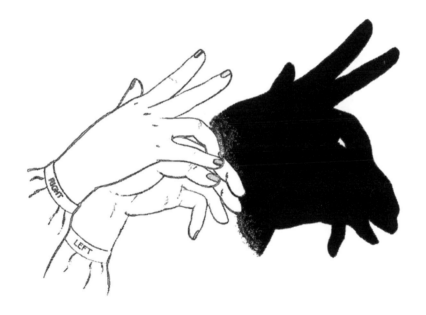

Suggestions:

Your hands take almost the same positions in making the shadow-picture of the rabbit's head that they did in making the goat's on the previous page. It is hard to form the animal's mouth. The fingers must be bent, for if they are stretched out, the rabbit will have a long lower jaw. The right hand will cover any opening which may be left between the thumb and the little finger. Move the right hand to the right so that the rabbit will close his eye, then bend the fingers so that he will seem to wave his ears.

Rabbit Head

Suggestions:

In making the shadow-picture of the donkey's head, the hardest part is setting the position of the index finger of the right hand. If you can make a good eye for your donkey, the rest of the picture will be simple. The fingers of both hands may be arranged in any way at all, if a sufficient space is left between them to represent the donkey's mouth. The fingers which form the nose and mouth should be kept tight together. Do not let the light shine on them in a way that you can recognize the shadow of a particular finger.

Donkey Head

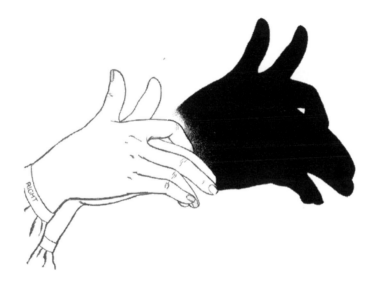

Suggestions:

Keep the long second finger of the right hand directly behind the index finger so that the nose in the picture will be an unbroken shadow of the two fingers. By raising the thumb of your right hand to touch the little finger of your left hand, you can make the lady close her eye. If you want to have it seem as if she is talking, make her lips move by raising the little finger and the ring finger. Don't bend the fingers that make the nose.

Old Lady or Curmudgeon

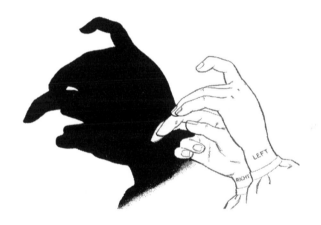

Suggestions:

When you open and close the mouths of your shadow-picture figures to make them seem as if they are talking, speak the words for them. If you have committed any little pieces to memory, let your shadow people "speak" them. If you make one figure, and then let someone make another to appear opposite yours, the two shadow-pictures will seem to be engaged in conversation. If you learn to fix your fingers so that the lips of the shadow-picture figures move naturally, it is great fun to hear the old man tell a story.

Old Man's Head with Cap

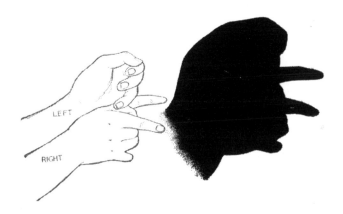

Suggestions:

Let the thumb of your left hand hold the two middle fingers of your right hand against the palm. In this way it is possible to keep all your fingers held closely in position. If your light is not very strong, the shadow will not be distinct, and in this picture it will be difficult to make the outlines sharp for the lady's mouth so you can make her talk. This one is hard to show in action, as it is too easy to move your hands a little and make a completely different shadow.

This character looks very much like Judy, of the Punch and Judy puppet team, well-known around the world in the early 1900's. Later, you will see how to represent both Punch and Judy, and you will be able to thrill and impress your parents and friends with your knowledge of Victorian-age entertainment!

Old Biddy (Judy)

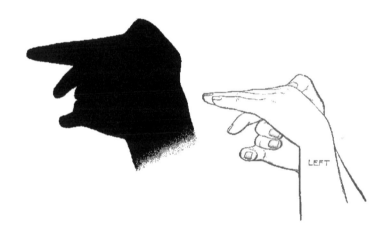

Suggestions:

This one will take a little practice and will improve your finger control. It is not at all easy to make the mouth of the shadow-picture devil! To allow suitable space to represent the mouth, the tip of the ring finger and the tip of the long second finger must be pressed tightly against the palm. Try to keep your fingers from slipping out of place. The lower part of the right hand must be tilted away from the light. The little finger and the ring finger of the left hand may be either doubled up or stretched out across the back of your right hand.

The Devil!

Suggestions:

If your only difficulty in making the devil's image was keeping your little finger in place, this picture of the Indian should be easy. With the exception of the little finger, your right hand is in the same position as for a devil. By bending the index finger of the right hand, you will cause the Indian's nose to grow shorter. Move the fingers of your left hand so that the Indian will seem to shake his feathers. Raise the ring finger and little finger of the left hand and make him "shout" his war-cries.

Indian Chief

Suggestions:

In making the pictures of this book, it doesn't really matter whether the light strikes the front or the back of the hands if the fingers are arranged properly to cast the right shadow. You will observe that the right hand on this page is in exactly the same position as the left hand on the next page. As we saw at the beginning of the book, when we made the picture of the rabbit, all shadows can be reversed simply by using the right hand in place of the left, and the left for the right. Here we learn how to reverse the positions of the hand.

Knave with Feathered Hat

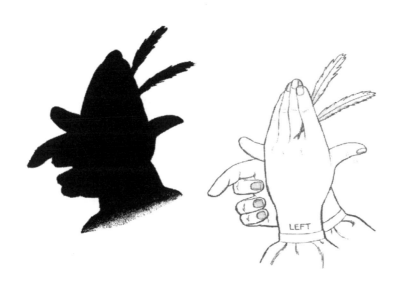

Suggestions:

You don't have to use both hands to make a shadow-picture man. A cardboard can be cut in almost any shape to form a hat, then held in the left hand where the fingers will make the nose and the mouth. If you hold your right hand a little farther from the light than you are holding your left, a smaller shadow will be cast, and the man will have a hand of his own. You can make him scratch his nose, lift a glass to his lips, or use his hands in whatever way you wish!

Witch

Suggestions:

Again, both hands can be arranged exactly as they were for the last shadow-picture—and any other form of cardboard cut-out used. Here we have the old man in his night cap! Remember that the shadow will look more lifelike if you cut an "eye" in the cardboard. However, if you intend to use your right hand so that the man will move his hat in any way, it is better not to let him have an eye. If he has an eye, each time you move the cardboard hat the eye will move about also. That would be a little weird!

Jester

Suggestions:

The left hand is still in the same position as it was when the last shadow-picture was made, but here we have cut our piece of cardboard in the shape of a woman's head instead of a man's hat. You can make any kind of a shadow person you desire if you simply take your scissors and cut the cardboard in the proper shape. Let the lady here fan herself. While you are making her open and close her mouth, bend your forefinger just a little. This will cause the lady to move her nose and the effect is really funny.

Old Maid

Suggestions:

A cardboard could be cut in the shape of a soldier's hat and held between the index finger and the thumb of the left hand. The expression on the soldier's face will depend entirely upon the positions of the four fingers of your right hand. By bringing the little finger closer to the palm you will take away his beard. By extending the index finger you will make his nose grow longer. By lowering the ring finger and the little finger you can cause the man's mouth to open.

Musketeer

Suggestions:

This drawing shows what can be accomplished if you use the cardboard cut-outs in making shadow-pictures. The figure shows the result of making changes in the right hand position suggested in the previous, musketeer example.

See how very different the shadows are. If you would cut out enough cardboard hats you could make the shadows represent many different characters, and so act out a little play. The two shown look like the Punch and Judy show puppets that were discussed a few pages back. It would be easy to put on a very animated show using these two characters.

Punch & Judy

Suggestions:

Does this picture seem strange? Why is that?

Since the right hand is held as near the light as the left, the man's hand is as large as his head! When you make a complete figure with one hand and then use the shadow which the other hand casts to represent the figure's hand, do not forget to keep that hand farther away from the light so that it will cast a smaller shadow.Be sure to make the hands of your shadow people smaller than their heads.

Scholar, Headmaster

Suggestions:

To make the horse's head narrow, keep your fingers flat in the light so the three fingers look more like one.

Move your left arm slowly up and down, bending it at the elbow, so that your horse will appear to be galloping. Jerk the right hand backward and make the jockey bring the horse to a walk. When the jockey is moving, keep the ring finger and the little finger of the right hand close behind the long second finger.

Horse Race with Jockey

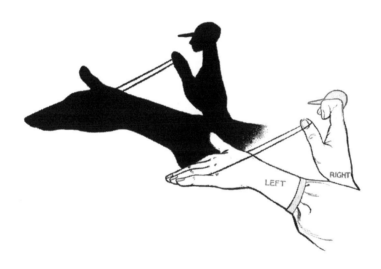

Suggestions:

Instead of holding the cardboard boat in your left hand, you can stand it on top of a book at the edge of a table. The book will cast a shadow which can represent the water with the fish at the end of the line behind the book so it doesn't cast a shadow. Your fisherman can then be seen patiently waiting for a bite. You can jerk the line a little with your left hand from behind the book. Then let the fisherman, after struggling hard, pull the little fish up triumphantly and drop him in the boat.

Fisherman in Boat

Watch for new books from BeachHouse Books
at www.beachhousebooks.com

PO Box 7151
Chesterfield, MO 63006-7151
(636) 394-4950

beachhousebooks.com
Books for the fun of it

Made in the USA
Lexington, KY
17 September 2012